How To Convince Your Parents You Can...

Care For A Pet Chameleon

Jim Whiting

Mitchell Lane
PUBLISHERS

P.O. Box 196
Hockessin, Delaware 19707
Visit us on the web: www.mitchelllane.com
Comments? email us: mitchelllane@mitchelllane.com

Printing   1   2   3   4   5   6   7   8   9

A Robbie Reader/How to Convince Your Parents You Can...

Care for a Pet Chameleon
Care for a Pet Chimpanzee
Care for a Pet Mouse
Care for a Pet Snake
Care for a Pet Tarantula

Library of Congress Cataloging-in-Publication Data
Whiting, Jim, 1943–
    Care for a pet chameleon / by Jim Whiting.
        p. cm. — (A Robbie reader)
    Includes bibliographical references and index.
    ISBN-13: 978-1-58415-605-5 (library bound)
    1. Chameleons as pets—Juvenile literature. I. Title.
SF459.C45W48 2007
639.3'95—dc22
                                                                        2007000807

ABOUT THE AUTHOR: Jim Whiting has been a remarkably versatile and accomplished journalist, writer, editor, and photographer for more than 30 years. As a youngster, Jim had several American chameleons (see page 25) as pets and enjoyed them a great deal. Mr. Whiting has written and edited about 250 nonfiction children's books. He lives in Washington State with his wife and two teenage sons.

PHOTO CREDITS: Cover, pp. 7, 8, 19, 28—© 2008 JupiterImages Corporation; pp. 4, 10—AFP/Getty Images.

PLB

TABLE OF CONTENTS

Words in **bold** type can be found in the glossary.

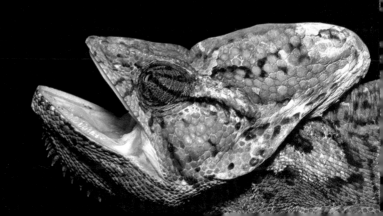

The Picasso panther chameleon is becoming a very popular pet in the United States. Chameleons shoot out their tongue at very high speeds in order to capture their prey. A suction cup at the end holds the prey while the chameleon brings it back to its mouth. Its tongue may be as long as its entire body.

 **Chapter One**

SO YOU THINK YOU WANT A PET CHAMELEON?

Chameleons (kuh-MEE-lee-uns) are nature's "quick-change artists." These lizards can change color in just a few seconds. Many people believe chameleons change color to blend into their surroundings so that they can hide from **predators** (PREH-duh-turs). While their colors may help **camouflage** them, chameleons can't change colors to hide.

There are two reasons that chameleons change color. One is to adjust their body temperature. The other is to show their feelings.

Chameleons are members of the reptile family. This family includes snakes, lizards, alligators, and turtles. Reptiles are cold-blooded. They do not produce their own body heat. Instead, most reptiles bask in the sun to get warm, and they rest in water or in the shade to cool down again.

Chameleons control their body heat by changing colors. Dark colors absorb more heat than light colors. Light colors reflect the sun's rays, so light-colored things don't get as warm as those with dark colors. During the heat of the day, the chameleon turns a light color. In the cool early morning or late evening, it turns darker.

Chameleons also change colors to show their feelings. When they get angry, their skin will get brighter. Sometimes colorful spots and lines will appear. Males use bright colors to attract females.

Sometimes two chameleons will have a fight. The fight usually doesn't last very long. When a chameleon gives up, it turns dull brown. This change tells the other chameleon that it doesn't want to fight anymore.

A similar color change sometimes happens to humans. People who are angry or embarrassed get red in the face. They don't try to. It just happens.

Many people like to keep chameleons as pets. They enjoy watching these fascinating animals. The chameleon's ability to change colors is one reason. Another reason is that they have an unusual appearance. Some male chameleons have horns on the front of their head. Chameleons are also among the best climbers in nature, and watching them climb can be spellbinding. Sometimes they will even hang upside down from a branch.

Chameleons eat insects and worms. It is entertaining to watch them feed. They have a long tongue with a sticky suction cup at the end for trapping prey. One moment their prey may be sitting on a leaf or branch, and the next moment it will be

A chameleon has captured an insect snack.

gone. In an instant, the chameleon can whoosh out its tongue, capture the prey, and bring it back into its mouth. It happens faster than the human eye can follow. After a while, pet chameleons may even feel comfortable enough to take food from its owner's hand.

Does all this sound like fun? Perhaps you have considered owning a chameleon as a pet, and all you

After you have owned a chameleon for a while, you may be able to feed it by hand.

have to do is convince your parents that you can. If so, there is something you have to keep in mind. Chameleons are not easy to care for. In fact, many authorities don't think chameleons are good pets for children.

However, for some children, chameleons may make ideal pets. You will learn a lot if you successfully raise a chameleon. You will be entertained. You will develop a sense of responsibility. It all depends on how much work you are willing to do.

A male Jackson's chameleon watches its three-week-old baby climb onto a branch. This baby may grow to be about a foot long. Chameleons can't change their colors when they are this young.

Chapter Two 2

ABOUT CHAMELEONS

Most wild chameleons live in Africa. Many of them are native to Madagascar, a large island off the eastern coast of Africa. A few live in the Middle East, in southern Europe, and in India. No chameleons live in the wilds of North or South America. Nearly all of them live in forests and jungles, where there are lots of trees and bushes in which they can live.

One of the obvious features of a chameleon is its long tail, which can be as long as its body. The tail is often used to help the chameleon climb branches. When the chameleon isn't using its tail, it coils it up neatly.

Its front and back feet are shaped like the letter Y. It uses them like tongs to grip tree branches. Sharp claws also help them hold on. With their powerful feet, chameleons can hang upside down for a long time.

However, these feet aren't **adapted** for living on the ground. Chameleons can't run very fast, and most of them don't like being on the ground. They are much more comfortable in a tree or bush.

Another interesting thing about chameleons is their eyes. They bulge out on each side of their head. Each eye can operate independently of the other. For example, one eye can look forward while the other eye looks sideways.

Their eyes help them hunt for prey. Chameleons remain motionless for long periods of time. Their eyes scan the surroundings. Eventually one eye will spot something to eat. Then both eyes focus on the prey. Using both eyes together is called binocular (buh-NAH-kyoo-lur) vision. It helps the chameleon see exactly how far away the prey is located. That way it can use its tongue accurately.

You can test binocular vision yourself. Cover one eye and look at an object a few feet away with your other eye. Reach forward and try to touch it. It's hard to tell how distant the object is. Then open both eyes. Now you have a much clearer picture of how far away the object is.

Chameleons are **solitary** creatures. They don't like to share their territory with other chameleons. The only time they get together is to mate. Then they split up.

For most chameleons, the male will fertilize the female's eggs. The female lays about 20 to 30 eggs in the soil beneath the trees. When the baby chameleon is ready to hatch, it uses a special sharp tooth to cut its way out of the egg. This egg tooth falls off soon after the hatchling emerges.

Chameleons grow rapidly when they are young, but their skin does not

funFACTS

Chameleon eggs take a long time to hatch. Most need between five and nine months. A few take longer than a year.

Female chameleons change color when they are almost ready to lay eggs. Their color change tells the males to stay away from them.

grow with them. When the chameleon's skin grows tight, the animal has to **molt** to get rid of it. It rubs against a rock or other rough surface, and the skin begins to flake off. Soon it is entirely gone, and new skin is revealed. It is a little loose at first, giving the young chameleon room to grow. Eventually this new skin also gets tight. Then the chameleon molts again.

Many chameleons don't like to be held. It scares them. Chameleons turn black when they are frightened.

Always wash your hands before and after you handle your pet chameleon. Lizards can carry salmonella (sal-muh-NEL-uh), a germ that causes serious disease.

 **Chapter Three**

CHOOSING A PET CHAMELEON

Chameleons are sold by two types of suppliers. One type of supplier raises chameleons in captivity. The other type captures animals that were born in the wild.

If you would like to buy a pet chameleon, you will be much better off buying one that has been born and bred in captivity. Wild-born chameleons don't easily adjust to being pets. The change from living in the wild to living in a cage makes them very stressed, which is harmful for chameleons. They will have traveled thousands of miles to their new home, which also increases the chance for serious injury. Wild-born chameleons are not guaranteed to be in good health. They are morely likely to have diseases and contain **parasites** (PAH-ruh-syts).

Captive-born chameleons, on the other hand, are used to the limited **habitat** (HAH-bih-tat) of a cage. They are much more likely to be healthy and not to carry diseases.

There are several things to look for in buying a chameleon. Its eyes should be bulging. Avoid any chameleon whose eyes are sunken.

Look at the tail. Healthy chameleons have a tail that clearly has muscle on it. If the tail appears to be simply skin and bones, bypass the animal.

Chameleons should seem alert and active. Watch them long enough to make sure that they can change their colors and become brighter.

Some experts think it is better to choose a male for a pet. Males are likely to be stronger and to live longer. Their nutritional needs are somewhat simpler. On the other hand, females are usually less aggressive. At some point, the female has to lay eggs. You'll need to provide an area in the cage where she can do that. If a female doesn't lay her eggs, she will retain them in her body, where they can cause serious internal damage.

Don't even think about putting two chameleons in the same cage. If you want two, consider a male and female—but be sure to keep them in separate cages except for breeding.

It's best if you spend some time setting up your new pet's living quarters before you bring it home. Moving from the place where it has been raised to a new environment is going to be very stressful. You

Veiled chameleons are the most common chameleon pets. They reproduce well in captivity.

don't want to have to keep your pet waiting while you set up its new home.

The most important thing you'll need to buy for your new chameleon is the container. Some authorities recommend a glass cage, while others suggest one that is entirely mesh. Mesh keeps the chameleon from seeing its reflection. Sometimes it can mistake this reflection for another chameleon, making it want to fight.

The cage should be wide enough to allow the chameleon to hide in the back. The safer it feels, the less stress it will feel. Reducing stress is very important in helping to give your pet a long life.

You will need a source of light. Fluorescent light is the best because it is the closest to real sunlight.

You'll need a dependable source of heat. Many chameleons like a very warm basking area. When they are warm enough, they'll go to a cooler part of the cage.

You'll also have to provide plants and branches so that your pet can have plenty of places to climb and to hide. Plants perform another function. Chameleons won't drink water from a bowl. They lick moisture off the plant leaves.

The right front foot of this horned chameleon clearly shows its Y-shape. The shape of its feet helps the chameleon keep a firm grip on branches as it moves around.

Especially in the beginning, don't handle your new pet. Chameleons don't enjoy physical contact. Never try to pry your pet off a branch or anything else it's trying to grip. Rough handling will cause stress and can possibly injure your pet. Wash your hands before and after handling any chameleon.

Your equipment should be of high quality. Although it can be fairly expensive, you definitely don't want to buy the cheapest. Chameleons in captivity are very delicate. You want to give your new pet the best chances for survival.

Chameleons need lots of branches in their cage. They also need plants because they don't drink water from bowls. Instead, they lick water from the leaves. You will need to clean your chameleon's cage every day.

 **Chapter Four**

CHAMELEON CARE

Think carefully about where to put your new pet's container. You don't want it to be where a lot of people or animals will pass it on a constant basis. To the chameleon, every passage represents a possible predator. That will make it very stressed.

You also don't want a lot of direct sunlight. The amount of heat can build up and make the container even hotter than it needs to be. A little early morning sun or late afternoon sun is the best. It is vital to lower the temperature at night, but it can't get too cold. A safe temperature range is 80 to 90 degrees Fahrenheit (27 to 32 degrees Celsius) during the day, and the mid-70s Fahrenheit (24 degrees Celsius) at night.

Ventilation and **humidity** are very important. The forest environments of chameleons are naturally very humid. You have to maintain the same conditions in the pet's container. You also need to provide a constant source of water. You can either spray the plants in the container at least two or three times each day, or you can install an automatic sprinkler.

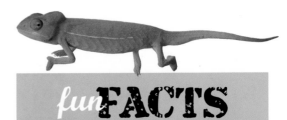

fun**FACTS**

When snakes molt, their old skin comes off in one long piece. Chameleons molt by losing their skin in several smaller sections.

Chameleons are active during the day and sleep at night. In your pet's cage, you'll have to turn the lights on in the morning and off in the evening—every day. A timer is a good investment, because it can be set to automatically turn the lights on and off at certain hours. It will provide a regular schedule that will help your pet. And if you forget, your pet won't suffer any damage.

Chameleons eat a lot of insects, such as crickets, caterpillars, and flies, every day. Their prey food has to be alive or they won't touch it. Pet stores usually have feeder insects, but the constant trips can be time-consuming. For that reason, you may have to raise your own food, such as houseflies.

It's important that the food be nutritious, so you'll have to give the insects regular dietary supplements. The need for maintaining a constant and nutritious food supply is one of the biggest drawbacks to owning a chameleon. It's almost as if you have another set of pets to take care of.

With so many pet requirements, you can't just go away and leave your chameleon. If you do go on vacation, it's important to find someone trustworthy to take care of your pet.

Reliable **veterinary** (VEH-truh-nayr-ee) care is essential. Many veterinarians don't treat **exotic** (ek-ZAH-tik) pets such as chameleons. It is important to find one that does. Your pet needs to be checked by a professional on a regular basis.

Does all this sound like a lot of work? You bet! Is it worth it? That's a decision you will have to make for yourself.

Many people confuse anoles with chameleons. This green Carolina anole, which is eating a dronefly, is native to the United States.

Chapter Five 5

HOW ABOUT AN AMERICAN CHAMELEON?

Now that you know a little more about chameleons, you'll be able to make a better decision about whether to own one. You know how much fun a healthy chameleon can offer. You also know that in captivity, chameleons are very fragile and can be hard to raise. Your parents almost certainly will have to help you. Even if they are willing, you still may not want to put in the amount of time that chameleons require. There is nothing wrong with that.

In the end, you may decide that you don't want to buy a chameleon after all. But if you are fascinated by animals that change colors, there is another possibility.

You may want to consider buying what is often called an American chameleon. The name is misleading. These animals aren't really chameleons. They are anoles (uh-NOH-leez). Like chameleons, they change their color, and they don't directly control these color changes. Unlike chameleons, though, anoles occur naturally in the United States. Most of them live in the South, where the climate is usually warm and humid.

Anoles still require a lot of careful attention and the same type of fairly expensive container and accessories. Yet they aren't as delicate as chameleons. Also, you can have two or three anoles in the same cage, as long as only one of them is a male. Having several can make them especially entertaining. Almost certainly at least one of them will be stalking prey or showing off its climbing ability. You can even combine anoles with other types of small reptiles or **amphibians** (am-FIH-bee-uns), giving you an interesting assortment of animals.

Like chameleons, anoles shed their skin. Molting enables them to grow.

Like chameleons, anoles molt. Also like chameleons, their skin comes off in several pieces. They may tug at the old skin to help pull it off. Sometimes they may even eat the old skin.

Anoles have different kinds of feet than chameleons. While anoles are just as agile in climbing branches, their toes stick to things instead of gripping. They can stick to the sides of glass aquariums. Watching them scurry up and down the smooth surface can be very entertaining.

They also don't seem to mind being handled. In the summer, you can take them out of their cage, put them on a window screen that has a lot of bugs on it, then sit back and watch them enjoy feeding on the insects.

Anoles can be a good first step to taking care of chameleons. If you successfully raise anoles for a couple of years, then you'll be much better prepared for a pet chameleon. And as many successful chameleon owners will tell you, it may be the most fascinating pet you'll ever own.

Good luck!

FIND OUT MORE

Books

Cowley, Joy. *Chameleon, Chameleon*. New York: Scholastic Press, 2005.

Garcia, Eulalia. *Chameleons: Masters of Disguise*. Milwaukee, Wisconsin: Gareth Stevens Publishing, 1997.

Glaser, Jason. *Chameleons*. Mankato, Minnesota: Bridgestone Books, 2006.

Jenkins, Marty. *Chameleons Are Cool: Read and Wonder*. Cambridge, Massachusetts: Candlewick, 2001.

Lodge, Alison. *Clever Chameleon*. Cambridge, Massachusetts: Barefoot Books, 2005.

Mara, W.P. *Chameleons*. Mankato, Minnesota: Capstone Press, 1996.

Stefoff, Rebecca. *Chameleon*. New York: Benchmark Books, 2007.

Works Consulted

Bartlett, Richard, and Patricia Pope Bartlett. *Chameleons: Everything About Selection, Care, Nutrition, Diseases, Breeding, and Behavior*. Hauppauge, New York: Barron's, 1995.

Schmidt, Wolfgang, Klaus Tamm, and Erich Wallikewitz. *Chameleons*. Philadelphia: Chelsea House Publishers, 1998.

Stein, Sara. *Great Pets!* North Adams, Massachusetts: Storey Kids, 2003.

FIND OUT MORE

Chameleons Online
http://www.chameleonsonline.com
McLeod, Lianne. "Choosing a Chameleon as a Pet."
http://exoticpets.about.com/cs/chameleons/a/
    chameleonbasics.htm
Chameleon Corral
http://www.chameleoncorral.com/htm/about.htm
Kids and Reptiles
http://www.chameleonsdish.com/kids.htm
Anoles
http://members.tripod.com/mistergecko0/id4.htm
Kaplan, Melissa. "Anoles."
http://exoticpets.about.com/od/anoles/

Web Addresses
Chameleon Rescue
http://magma.nationalgeographic.com/ngexplorer/0210/
    games/game.cgi
Cooper, Sharon Katz. "Chameleons."
http://magma.nationalgeographic.com/ngexplorer/0210/
    articles/mainarticle.html
Colors of a Chameleon
http://www.kidzworld.com/site/p1740.htm

GLOSSARY

adapted (uh-DAP-tid)—adjusted to a different environment.

amphibians (am-FIH-bee-uns)—animals that live at least part of their lives on land and another part in water.

camouflage (KAA-muh-flahj)—disguising one's appearance in order to hide.

exotic (ek-ZAH-tik)—very unusual; rare.

habitat (HAH-buh-tat)—the area in which an animal lives.

humidity (hyoo-MIH-dih-tee)—the amount of moisture in the air.

molt—to cast off an outer layer of skin.

parasites (PAH-ruh-syts)—creatures that attach themselves to and live off other creatures.

predators (PREH-duh-turs)—animals that try to catch other animals for food.

solitary (SAH-lih-tay-ree)—by oneself; alone.

veterinary (VEH-truh-nayr-ee)—dealing with preventing or curing animal diseases or injuries.

INDEX